SIMPLE MACHINES

SCREWS ARE MACHINES

DOUGLAS BENDER

A Crabtree Roots Plus Book

CRABTREE
Publishing Company
www.crabtreebooks.com

School-to-Home Support for Caregivers and Teachers

This book helps children grow by letting them practice reading. Here are a few guiding questions to help the reader with building his or her comprehension skills. Possible answers appear here in red.

Before Reading:

- What do I think this book is about?
    - *I think this book is about screws.*
    - *I think this book is about how screws are used.*
- What do I want to learn about this topic?
    - *I want to learn how a screw can be useful to me.*
    - *I want to learn about the different sizes of screws.*

During Reading:

- I wonder why...
    - *I wonder why a screw has a head.*
    - *I wonder why screws can be used to hold things together.*
- What have I learned so far?
    - *I have learned that screws have threads.*
    - *I have learned that some screws are big, and some are small.*

After Reading:

- What details did I learn about this topic?
    - *I have learned that a lightbulb has a screw on one end.*
    - *I have learned that a screwdriver is a tool that turns a screw.*
- Read the book again and look for the vocabulary words.
    - *I see the word **threads** on page 9 and the word **screwdriver** on page 20. The other vocabulary words are found on page 23.*

This is a **screw**.

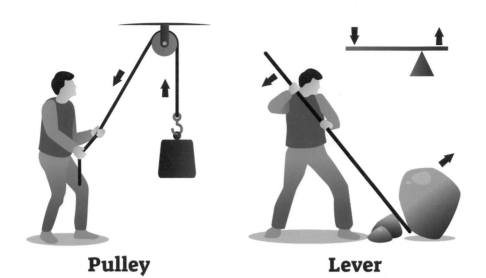

Pulley　　　　　**Lever**

Screw

It is one of six
simple machines.

Wedge

Inclined Plane

Wheel and Axle

Simple machines have few or no moving parts.

A screw has two parts.

It has a **head**.

threads

It also has **threads**.

Screws help us hold things together.

propeller

Screws also help us move things.

propeller

A **propeller** is a
type of big screw.

Some screws are small. Tiny screws hold a pair of glasses together.

The lid on a jar is a screw.

A **lightbulb** has a
screw on one end.

Taylor screws in a lightbulb.

A **screwdriver** helps to turn a screw!

Word List
Sight Words

a	hold	some
also	is	things
are	it	this
big	move	to
can	moving	together
end	no	turn
few	on	two
has	one	us
head	or	
help	parts	
helps	small	

Words to Know

 head

 lightbulb

 propeller

 screw

 screwdriver

 simple machines

 threads

CRABTREE
Publishing Company

SIMPLE MACHINES
SCREWS
ARE MACHINES

Written by: Douglas Bender
Designed by: Rhea Wallace
Series Development: James Earley
Proofreader: Janine Deschenes
Production coordinator
 and Prepress technician: Katherine Berti
Print coordinator: Katherine Berti
Educational Consultant: Marie Lemke M.Ed.

Photographs:
Shutterstock: Tawansk: cover, p. 1; looka: p. 3, 23; Nikita G. Bernadsky: p. 6;
 Yuriy Boyko: p. 8, 13; Rynio Productions: p. 9, 13; Juice Flair: p. 11; Shuravio7:
 p. 12-13; Piece of Cake: p. 15; Piece of Cake: p. 15; Hazel AK: p. 17; azazello
 photostudio: p. 18, 23; Digitalpen: p. 19; JaCrispy: p. 20, 23

Library and Archives Canada
Cataloguing in Publication

CIP available at Library and Archives Canada

Library of Congress
Cataloging-in-Publication Data

CIP available at Library of Congress

Crabtree Publishing Company

www.crabtreebooks.com   1-800-387-7650   Printed in the U.S.A./CG20210915/012022

Published in the United States
Crabtree Publishing
347 Fifth Avenue, Suite 1402-145
New York, NY, 10016

Published in Canada
Crabtree Publishing
616 Welland Ave.
St. Catharines, ON, L2M 5V6